Woodshedding

S.E. Venart | Woodshedding

Brick Books

Library and Archives Canada Cataloguing in Publication

Venart, Sarah, 1968-
    Woodshedding / S.E. Venart.

Poems.
ISBN 978-1-894078-61-0

    I. Title.

PS8643.E53W66 2007   C811'.6   C2007-902767-9

We acknowledge the support of the Canada Council for the Arts, the
Government of Canada through the Book Publishing Industry Development
Program (BPIDP), and the Ontario Arts Council for their support of our
publishing program.

Cover image: "Head with Birds" 2003, 24 x 24 inches, charcoal, ink, graphite,
Xerox-transfer, oil and collage on paper on canvas, by Stas Orlovski.

Author photo by: Dr. Douglas Hamilton.

The book is set in Minion and Birch.

Design and layout by Alan Siu.

Printed by Sunville Printco Inc.

Brick Books
431 Boler Road, Box 20081
London, Ontario N6K 4G6
www.brickbooks.ca

For Elizabeth Venart

Woodshedding *vi* [fr. English slang *woodshed,* from woodsheds being formerly used to administer sound parental thrashings](1936): arduous and solitary rehearsal; spontaneous or improvised singing.

"I want to see everything, I don't care how hard it is."
— Ernest Oberholtzer

Contents

Woodshedding

Gardens, Cars, and Living Rooms

Postcards to You

We Return from Running

Woodshedding

Wake

There are sudden canopies
of silence between the low tones

of speedboats, between the water-skiers'
whoops and peels,

their white arcs on the waves.
We bob there, treading

water, waiting for the wake
to roll us

back to shore. You remember
waiting like this, don't you?

When it comes, the surprise
is that it's in you, lifting.

Woodshedding Is (a Found Poem)

The most productive and fulfilling activity you can choose
to do. How society began. A sort of jam session. The nuts.
All the proof you'll need. Time spent in a hole or a well,
depending. The work. Meant for your ears only.
About honing technique. A waste of time
if you don't get up and blow. Evidently
on track. Out of the way. The new fromage.
Further proof that you bring out the worst
in yourself. A startlingly moving tribute
on a small face. What you may call it. When you get in
a mood. Spending the day seeing what you can get
out of one note. The process of getting details down, all
it's cracked up to be, the proof you need, coming
to, required, tender, the answer if you hit a wall, my friend.

Similes on Dark Days

See? Not so real, not so enduring—
like an eclipse, or less,
like the dent the dark
can make against the moon.
I mean, it's not as if this mood
wipes out your soul.
It only masks it for a while.

Double Wide

I'm cat sitting this afternoon,
reading *Sex and the Single Girl*
in a sun-heated armchair
while Marlon purrs,
schmoozes about my ankles.
He's not lovely; basically
your average footstool with a shitty ass,
equivalent in cat-weight to
that man who when he died had to be crane-
lowered by piano box to the street below.
In other words, this cat is large,
so when an orange cat—dwarf
in comparison—appears at the window,
it's a surprise to all concerned
that Marlon traverses several rooms,
heaves himself mid-air
to body-check the glass.

I think the building shifts
slightly to the left. On her side
of the glass, the dwarf falls off
the world. Marlon swaggers to his food dish,
lies down to eat his dinner.
Splayed on the linoleum he looks
like the photo
of the largest man on earth—
the one taken in a Double Wide
face down, in Arkansas, the body
like two continents, spreading
side by side. What struck me most—
and Marlon would agree with me on this—

how human, ineffectual
the tea towel someone laid
for modesty across
his great divide.

Sand Crabs

The dog gives you some happiness—
at low tide upending
sand crabs that have clawed their way under the surf.

With crazy words of warning
in your head—like, *You never truly know*
how good or safe you are—it's surprising

you still see beauty, catch it
in the scissoring
of crickets in the Marram grass,

the flashing red light
on the answering machine
as you turn sideways through the door.

Another morning, after
the dog's let out and fed,
you don't bother making up

the bed, folding clothes, facing yourself
brushing your teeth. What a thing absence is
to live with. How shrugged the cover gets

with you alone, the jumbled peak
your hand is as it attempts the miracle
of pens. The dog

just doesn't get how anyone
could choose one chair to sit
and sit, the sun's slow sidle

taking sides against the house, how the page
is emptied by eraser. She prefers to pace
or chew pink balls between her teeth.

Without uncertainty, it disappears—
this need to scuttle in, clamp down, become
a dark edge in a house.

Peas Bay

Expecting brawny and brave surfers,
I find the crust of reef empty

except for hollow caravans
of holidayers, and the raw face

of the ocean. I watch this view and wait
for it to watch me back. You said

it's simple to see,
but I can't tell

if the ninth or seventh wave
is making a clean break,

wanting to be taller,
lighter, more majestic—

today, every wave falls oddly on this shore,
revealing tumult, truly seen,

outside hope, outside routine.

Hawthornden Journal

This castle is too much a gallery, it makes me mute.
Strolling past the portraits of prolific writers
I feel like occupation should be easier than this.
Victorian hunting cards frame my desk (reminder

of days when shooting parties slept in my bamboo bed,
washed briskly at my wash stand, pulled on red coats,
called hounds, climbed on horses, and fired at rusty foxes
sipping the edges of the Esk).

It's raining out, late autumn
confusion: cloudburst swapping places
intermittently with sun. Opening
a bamboo drawer, I look down

at my own distorted self—hand mirror
on green felt.
And in a spindly secretary
perched against the wall

a moth.
Alive, brown velvet, slowly opening
her wings revealing gold blue-spotted palms,
then snapping herself closed. I'm startled by her

flapping out. She heads towards the window,
where the latch won't budge. I know the damp
that shuts us in. And I remember warnings
as a kid, how touching wings forever grounds

these things. If I can't release her,
I can admire her kind of courage:
it's audible, the throb of wings
slows like a clock unwinding

in an empty house,
calling fewer and then
fewer hours. Outside, the Royal Mail
truck crunches into view. Lunch is placed outside

my door. I wait, as if waiting is the same
as wanting and shafts of light
will always be inserted
between the dark pulls of downpour.

Bat Walk

I

Heinz's man describes
himself with pride: *I'm a meat
and two veg man, myself—*

and no one laughs
but me and the Welsh poet,
who laughs at her potatoes.

Tonight, it's right we should escape
this place, the pursed disapproval
of our host, these tall grave castle walls,

so we go on a bat walk,
join a line of strangers, trailing
two-by-two into the woods.

Light lowers
to our sightline, the scraped-down sky
fades from blue to bruised.

We're busy
swatting flies that hum around
our arms in thirsty misery.

Like he's wearing a watch
synchronized with grace,
the first bat appears. No bigger

than an eye, masked mouse
in a winged suit. In swoops
another from the treeline

and we're mesmerized as witnesses
witnessing this lively duo
clear the air

snuffing out electric bugs,
no-see-ums and gnats
drunk on our riled wine.

II

Wow, you say. *How National Geographic.*
And I realize I'm taken with you
the way I once was taken

by my brother: how nonchalantly he
made moments that remain still
in the murky pocket of my heart. Once—equipped

with bread-bag parachute—
he floated a field mouse
from our barn roof.

We watched the tiny graceful swoop of its descent.
Once he trapped and skinned a chipmunk,
tanned its hide

to make a dollhouse rug, no bigger than
an eye patch. I want to be low-key here.
All *meat and veg*, short-circuiting

nostalgia, but I will always be a sister,
remembering
and crying. Each time I think of my brother,

I'll admit his darker times
flash in my head.
How we watched his pacing wear a trough

into the runner of our hall, a path
he made from basement
back to those of us still living

in our house. Down there he lit,
over the years, at least
three thousand cigarettes.

I wonder if illumination
was his secret antidote, a gesture
in a world of gestures that healed less.

Wind

After being jilted by a love who did not deserve your love,
a squall staining the bay deep grey, whipping last leaves, pushing

tree limbs toward the ground, you come over to the house
where I am house-sitting. We don't speak so much as sigh

into the pillows on the couch, overwhelmed by not knowing
what to say. The lack of answers transforms your face

into a five-year-old's, one I remember
from a windstorm back when we were still part

of a family living on a farm. Back then, the wind
seemed terrifying. Our older sisters thought

it was their job to teach us
fear is only overcome by being locked

into the fear itself. They shut you
outside first, leaning tall

as broomsticks behind each door.
Now we know that being locked in

to what's frightening
imbeds fear that much deeper. At the time, I wanted

to see what you would do
in case they turned on me.

I watched from an upstairs window while
you ran in circles on the lawn, hands covering your ears.

We still can't save each other—
instead we drink pot after pot of tea, pace

these windows, watch for clearings in the weather
when we hike along the beach, race for sand dollars

the tide pulls in, meander around grand empty houses
we adore but do not wish to own.

Collection

In the beach grasses, I picked sea peas, preferring smaller pods,
furred between my fingertips, the peas' hard seeds inside. And also wild

birds' eggs—forbidden, something sly, I hid them in birdcages
left rotting in fruit trees by someone who'd lived there

long before us. Some wood, some painted metal, one so small
my mother said it might be a cage used when travellers travelled

with their birds in steamships across the ocean, or
in trains that swept like an arm outstretched across the cornrowed prairie.

Satinwood, moulded brass feet, cutglass handle: in here I hid
the perfect white egg, pinkie-sized, under the nest

I did not know until last year belonged
to a pair of hummingbirds.

Twins from Koi

Strangers in a hostel room undertake the morning mime
of dressing without sound. From sleeping bags emerge
the twins from Koi. The first one shyly fastens up her bra
within the tent of her pyjama top.

Stark light from tall uncurtained windows falls
on the other twin. She sits unflinchingly and naked
on our stone floor. She knows we all are watching
as she lifts her bra's sheerness to her shoulders, shows us precisely

what her sibling veils within her veils. And when,
like a lasso from her knapsack, she unwinds
a long skirt, steps in its circumference, tiny hectic bells
along her hemline chime our room to life.

Substantia Nigra, Espalier...

Across the bay, light rises to illuminate
the shadowed surface of the reactor. Icicles
glance off the *Breeze Inn* sign

and bore into the snow. Closer,
the gunmetal hunch of underpass
is good, a weight unto itself.
But still, there is a wayward desperation

to the light that slips in empty pistils
through the blinds. In the nook, the sun
can't stop itself from clinging
to the paper scraps of lists: *Look up* substantia

nigra! *Look up espalier, photons,*
the origin of the question mark.
In other words, the world appears
to hold itself together. Except

in the grey hallway where keys
on key rings, running shoes,
and the storm door freeze
into their minor roles and wait.

Lanes

Up the road, three boys were hit
when their brother clipped
the corner of the driveway
fresh from his driving test.
My brother, almost forty,
delivers papers still.
At four in the morning, he discovers
men who do not like to sleep
asleep at their TVs, women
searching the lit pools
of bathroom mirrors
for their fallen faces—

I've decided fate
is a lofty thing. Myself,
I thought I'd marry
a man who could have been
the poster child for pot.
He smoked it while he taught
Croats and Serbs to speak
a common language.
Knowing better, he ran off to the Gulf Islands
where he grows marijuana in a milk truck.
He loves to ride
on BC Ferries stoned:
the wind holds him so firmly
he doesn't have to think
and humpbacks line up like they're picking
lanes to race the water.

Most mornings, I alternate
between love and distaste
just pulling back the sheet. The sun
overcoming me
as it climbs up and up the walls,
throwing light down on me as I bring
flesh and soul together, and fall
again into the moving traffic of myself.

Exercise

To learn what comes between the world
and you, move

beyond the window screen
to polished leaves. Beyond that even—

fractured clouds, rain, a balance tipping
the grey siphon of sky.

Still, no finish line.

And you call yourself a runner. As if
at your table, working

imagined muscles in your legs
is as good as running.

Distraction

Astounding how the walls correct themselves,
become tomorrow. How light upon the stairs
is mutiny—cast yellow
in its method towards dusk. On the lips
of coffee cups, the day

occurs even if I part with
conversation, shopping, and the like.
It whisks along—my difficulties snubbing words,
not enough of what is clear staying that way. Devotion
to the desk and chair elude me, words climb

from the dictionary and disappear, like
my own blown-over tracks
on stairwell and carpet.
And in the hem of windows—
my reckoning:

air curved full of motes, what is missing
plentiful. If only torpidity were easy,
another plot conceived in scot-free leisure—
dawn, say.
Instead, the heat-hazed strut of compulsion;
instead, the wearing down of want.

Woodshedding (Reprise)

You are *a sham and a low sham*. This lowness rears
in solitude. So low, it takes liberties with the coffee maker,
New Yorker cartoons, *Harper's* Index, your toothbrush,
and anything else that's helpless. At teatime the sun sinks

and your lowness sinks with it, as you steal cigarettes with *Oprah*
or *Dr. Phil*. Boiled water, tea bag, television—
these things come as cheap as pleasing.
But this is solitude. There's no one here to please.

Gardens, Cars, and Living Rooms

Power Lines

Travelling by station wagon: five children
in the back, the newest baby held on someone's knee.

The car gained momentum, sped down hills.
Over one tanned sister's shoulder I saw vivid fields

locked behind white lengths of birch. Wires loped
between attendant poles. Strapped into our seats,

we had in common things we couldn't get at.
Up on the wires, small birds alighted, fluttered off

as if together they'd all heard
the same charged message.

Uprising

Pushing ourselves up: our first revolt, raising
onto knees and fists, finding our grip
in carpet, corner table, crawling around
the rounded corners of our rec room.
We move jerkily then race then dance.
We push away beautifully. This new word

No! comes sprouting on our tongues. Meanwhile,
she stands empty-handed in the foyer.
No more buckles to clasp, ties to tie, hoods
to pull tight as alarm bells on our heads.
We're stalwart, gleaming in our red raincoats.
The door opens to grey light, rain bouncing off our arms

stretched out for balance. Oh, we wave back at her—
but our eyes are hooked on the sidewalk, far ahead.

We Are Happy

The holding pattern: the garden, our mother
draped on gold-flowered cushions
on the cedar deck chair. Behind her,
our lawn falls greenly to the wading pool.
Beyond the jagged dark of firs
wild birds bob on the branches.
Our father slings his arm up
to an empty feeder, taps around.
Those small birds eye his fingers
and flap away.

The windshield of the Volvo is where we learn
distance: not only a fixed tip
on that slender triangle the road is
and the signs, still and tall on the embankment,
but also words our parents whip, pointed
words, between the narrow back seat and the front.
Sometimes it is not enough to be still.
Our mother's cheeks lack rouge,
her hands are white caps on her knees.

Still there are evenings, drunk in our sunken
living room, when our mother sweeps in, kisses
our father hard on the mouth, and winks
at the line of us on the sofa, watching television.
Across from me, in the yellow conversation chair,
whatever my father was has fallen away. He's silent,
lips blurred red, a reflection
in his black-framed glasses of the TV screen
where a fast, long-legged bird honks his happy horn
but never truly outwits darkness.

These things are not explained,
but gradually life takes place
in gardens and cars and living rooms
where the moment isn't him anymore, isn't her.

Varsity Drive

We don't talk about the days you didn't get up,
a tent under the bedclothes, the bassinet beside you.
We missed you and came crawling from the foot of the bed,
slow bubbles through the thick blankets,
blinking up at your humped silence.

We never mention how in the late afternoon
you emerged to the dark kitchen, didn't see how we stared
whole minutes while you filled a mason jar with water,
stood at the window, your socks stretched empty,
hanging off your feet.

Or how we congregated in the basement,
planned ways to pull you out and sent the elected
to tug your dressing gown sleeve, remind you
how, the spring before, pregnant still and making jam,
you took our hands in a clasp, dipped each fist

in coloured wax, preserving our smallness to hang
on strings, now fading in the kitchen window.
Sometimes we were good enough to trick you
out of sadness. You would turn from the window's dusk, flick
the light switch and become

the softer mother we sought when we ran nightmare-driven,
sheets pulled over our heads, down the black length of the hall.
We don't say how it was
your name solid in our throats. Or tell how resolutely shut
our eyes were, running headlong through the house.

Canary

February being what it is,
you bring an old pair of binoculars
to the window, inspect the expected
paths of birds returning home.

Between unlikely sightings,
you like to be close to the stove.
In a butter-coloured jacket, you sing
to anything on radio,

punch down rising
loaves of bread while stirring
golden fruit peels
into a brandied jelly.

When you fly from the warmest room,
we look everywhere for you.
In the attic of our house,
we catch you, swinging

old valises down the hatch.
We look up, and you face us
like an animal that's trained to speak
but doesn't really like to.

Intimates

They argue in the cool,
fly-riddled bedroom while
down in the living room, we sit
on the floor, dry as nutshells.
We make twist-tie spiders and topple them
with green-eyed marbles; we don't utter a sound;
we're listening up the stairs
where need lives, the large need for us to be ready
for motion, for noise and the confession,
hers this time, *I am letting go, I have to let go*—
we'll willingly breathe it in,
like his pipe smoke or the moist air from her lace slips,
bras drying on hooks by the bath.

Her voice, the tight burn of it, teaches
again how the world is oiled only
with chance, not with hope—
our hope, or the hopes of the other
dismissed ones. Like the graduate student
who's been coming over for weeks now, the one
with the long hair, grey-rimmed glasses
who left our mother in the kitchen
to come down on his knees to play marbles
with us on our Oriental rug.
I for one carried on like his sister, an intimate.
In his absence, he's with me
and my spiders, my glass eyes,
my dry and silent downstairs.

Homecoming

The first night he goes missing, his absence
makes the house feel dislocated, heavy,
almost equal to the weight of his returned
sleeping body on our chesterfield

the next morning when we get up for school.
The next time he vanishes, it's the weekend.
We wait mostly in our beds, or sitting
in the square silence of the parquet hall.

He calls calmly on Monday
to tell us he'll be home for supper. We push
the afternoon along, love him even after this long trick
of disappearing. We have our table set, supper settled

in the oven. Our mother puts her earrings in, lights candles
as we hide scattered toys and shove into the hamper
a cluster of crayons, squares of construction
paper, a lump of dampish towels. We watch

the perfect golden hour pull its light across
the black neck of our drive. To make a game
of waiting those last minutes, we hide
under the stairs. In the dark, with hair licked flat

and good shoes on, we press against the patter
of our mother's ribs, listen for his engine
to cut out on the drive. When we lose all feeling
in our legs, we look up into the darkness

of her face, ask: *Can your body fall asleep like this?*
We have no room to worry until she answers: *I suppose so. Yes.*

Advantage: House

After this fight, our mother's victory is
to be alone behind the laundry door, folding
pastel baby sheets, sorting mismatched socks,
darning in frenzy.

Our father, restless with defeat, applies himself
to housework. He tugs light strings on and off in closets,
knocks on our hollow walls. In the sunlit pathway of our room,
he carries an undulating pile

of poster boards—*Kinds Of Horses, Solar System, How
Volcanoes Actually Erupt*—throws them in the trash.
Pausing to fix his dishevelled hair, he asks us for help
up in the attic, placing tin plates

of mouse poison on the beams. After, he lifts us
each up to the sink. While he rubs our fingernails with soap,
we see he's weeping. Not so much curious
as wonder-filled, we follow him

down to the basement. In the sauna he's begun to build
but hasn't finished yet, we watch him
pouring make-believe cold water
over make-believe hot stones.

Mackerel Clouds

All day clouds hang like thin bones in the sky.
We point up to ask: *What are those?*

Our mother and our father rub sunscreen
on each other or stare down at the sand.

Without looking up they know the answer:
mackerel clouds—forecasting rain.

Inside our cottage, warnings aren't
so clearly spelled; we can never learn

enough, so we lean out from our bunks
to ask each other: *Did you see if*

they laid their beach towels on the sand
together or apart?

The porch door claps one answer.
The Volvo revs, its headlights swipe our walls.

Blotting out the clouds, night falls
on top of evening.

My sister remembers
the rain, and how it did not come.

From where we lie, the black gap
on the driveway seems graceless

as a blunder.
We reach towards it anyway.

The Horse Trees

In O'Dell Park, we're the pack of children you see
As chaotic. But we know what we're doing.
We youngest five are stacked along that bench

Beneath the trees, fish and chip nests on our laps.
We eat with hands that have not been cleaned for days.
Our mother doesn't know this; the older sisters do.

They're the ones who wait and watch from
Trees we call The Horse Trees: twisted low
Limbs on which we ride as if we're riding horses.

The oldest sisters stand up on the branches, look down.
They watch us and they hover, they bounce and balance,
Arms strapped tight on each flat chest.

We think maybe we want to make the tall ones know
We really really love them. And we need them. Already
They've learned everything we're only old enough to see.

Accident

The Volvo spills us, all six of us
in pea coats, in wellingtons.

We're pointing like needles
all over the road.

We have broken things, inside
sounds aren't right.

Someone carries us to the ditch.
We are in the ditch, watching

the car, a green box
buzzing and bent like a hinge.

It had been a kind of home before
and now, on its side, it is not.

Panorama

We turned in our seats, watched sidewalks
ditch us, city leave us. Suburbs loomed

and then diminished. On each side of the highway,
foothills doled out their exact mauve knobs.

The sky beyond but not above us. Swathing
machines swallowed yellow walls, wheat

swooned and it fell over. Those first hours,
we were as pious as voyageurs or nuns.

We ate the halvah, sandwich halves, the pears.
The yellow dotted line we followed became

a long, tight rope. The next motel we stopped at
had to have a pool.

Chi Mi Frena

The island is our own, an inconvenient
province we visit each summer
as if visiting ensures it truly exists.

The pontoon shrugs us off
at dockside, recedes up the lake.
Everything is as we left it.

In the houseboat, records
wait upon the shelf, the old Victrola
winding up, Lucia's *Chi Mi Frena*
scratching at the speaker.

Light chooses moments, filters
through the spines
of evergreens, refracts off
tight pine cones on the path.

And when we float inside
the lake's wide lid, water presses
at our sides, holds us
like a luge.

Above, in the blue corridor
of sky, evening is falling. Fledgling
sparrows try their song, half finish, clear
the syrinx, start again.

This fissure in what sounds
familiar hurts somewhere.
A knob switches on and off
between our throats and hearts.

Lanterns

They're having adult cheeses with blue mould
and black crackers, red wine; someone puts
The Kingston Trio on the turntable; someone
takes it off, and we are sent to bed.

When they close our door, we turn on
flashlights, become a row of lanterns
in our beds. We can't leave night long enough
alone, how it alters and obscures our door
into a mouth, our walls sounding
boards for the world below: a panic-stricken
blender mixing sweet pink drinks,
our mother laughing, "God, that's rich!"—

I will never go to sleep. In my notebook,
I've begun a row of all the nouns I know:
sisters,
brother,
camouflage,
bed,
pillows,
chairs around the table—
I'm distracted when my brother jumps up,
runs the dark hall to the bathroom. My sisters
give up, turn off flashlights, and fall into their pillows.
In the lit circle of my page, my mother
drops four grapefruits in a silver grocer's scale,
taps each yellow head, adds one orange,
winks, "For the babe, who's still a babe in the woods
and won't know the difference."

My brother runs back down the dark hall—
noun, verb, adverb—
the world below continues. My mother laughs,
a pulse, its brightness squeezing past
the dark. I close myself so tight a window
appears inside me, framing
the breakfast table, grapefruits
on saucers, the bright half-lie of orange
on the baby's tray. Parading after this come
toast soldiers, eggs, the sunlit path to school.

Slide Show

In the dark, we line the couch,
watch motes shine like wayward
constellations in the bright triangle

of light. This next one shows
our northern hill, fixed electric fencing
frame two tiny specks upon it:

our red setter, our brother
with the set of wings he fashioned
out of plastic sheets and balsa.

Remember how he pumped
those long extended arms
and launched his run downhill?

The setter leaps. The wings
take giant breaths and catch
on what may be sunset or explosion.

Trampoline

Was it like that? Not first leap, nor
first fall, but the second
I am thrown back up

so quickly I'm convinced I see everything
birds see: the cul-de-sac an asphalt
bracelet. Broken elms and station wagons

strung like charms along it. The clubs of cedars
up the walk to this brick box I named
with my own mouth: *my* house. From up here,

home has no sides.
The roof's pitch sparkles in the sun
like nothing you imagine from the ground.

Chores

Half-nude in her bikini, our mother paces the channels
of our lawn, inspects how well we used the mower.
Imploding in the hammock, my sister and I
err on the side of caution, cover up
in sweatshirts and leggings.
The flower beds around the deck look sharp,
our destruction is our secret: at the dark edge
of the cedars, wildflowers
spewed like white paint, torn stems like green wires.

Super Light

After school, before dinner, we seek out
the last light of the veranda. Glassed-in,

curtained here and there by ferns, we sit
around our mother, the youngest

and the oldest sister get the window seats
beside her. Plain, bulky in our boots

and jeans, we have old Band-Aids
on our knees, our book bags marked with pens

and mud. In this lit green room, we want
to be different, as measured as her breathing.

Her gold-ringed fingers reach out,
wrap around her glass; its out-of-focus liquid swishes,

languid, side-to-side, and in one fragment
of a second, her wineglass splits the light,

and prisms dash, zooming up our faces.
We want to deserve this light, sit tight,

knees against our chests, but inside
we have these bells

trembling and pretending not to ring.
We want to be less eager, closer to what she is:

someone so refined she swallows all the space
around her, a world that's still and empty,

where dazzled dust can lucidly abide.
Is that what could absolve us?

We just want forgiveness,
a kind of super light.

At the Point

For me, is there always distraction?
Eyes lifting for menace—a seagull's
teasing swoop as I eat my packed snack
of pickled eggs and apples, scowl at

fishermen pulling from the dock.
I walk the sand paths leading
to the point, past silent campers in the fields,
dewed orange tarps, grass bristling

underfoot, take long sprints
through wind-pulled spruce, pines
branching out in whisks, eager
for joy or something. A loitering

radar on that blanched stretch
of beach, I dig sticks in sand, try to take cues
from this bay's wide mouth—
but I can hold nothing longer than a blip.

I am not happy. I can't stand
resignation, that sand just waiting
for the wipe of tide. The water's farther edge out there
is close enough, but never closer.

Seventeen's Song

We love dusk, dark skies getting darker, the echoes
we make running through empty lots, also apples
and apricots, eye contact, smiles between us
and old men on the street, between women
and us. We love driving home, parking just right.
Our mother's laughter in hallways and stairwells,
in the background of phone calls. We love dry socks,
our father who tells us to call, make sure we call,
young men walking us from cafés to parks, pulling
us to their laps, brushing our hair back
from our foreheads, looking at us like we're something
to look at, our mother's lemon cake glazed with sugar,
sugar itself. Without guilt, to sleep in the afternoon,
baby sisters who push at our sides when we read to them
or watch them watch television, how they think
what they see is real life.

We love being frightened when we know
we are safe, how we will drop the phone,
rush toward noise we don't know,
and find nothing, that relief.
We even love hospitals, our father perched
on that metal table, how he swung his legs
like a kid. Later, we have the same wonder
for typhoons, one rips the roof from our
bus shelter, wheels it out onto the street,
cicadas still clinging to the frame.

We love first person without knowing
what first person is, we love first person
plural even more. We love how, before bed,

our father says, *I'm off to the nest.*
We love our mother's milkshakes with tiger's milk,
we love fleece, friends calling from the street, *Hey, Mitten, wake up,*
we love hospitals, our father asking, *Move*
the car around front, park it well, how he shakes
the car keys like gifts—
and the babies we baby-sit, we wake them sometimes,
when we're lonely or something,
we don't know what to call it, we love sleep-giddy
babies watching with us the love scenes
on television we can watch without hiding
because no one is watching us watch,
we eat bowls of cereal, sugar-coated
like we don't get at home,
we love *Star* magazine, three lamps on
around us, pools of light on the road,
dark skies above that, clean and empty,
and purity, no one we know yet
broken.

Conversation Between a Father and a Daughter

What isn't spoken hangs.
Sways when pushed.

On her side, fists duked. On his, head tucked
like a question mark. Because he is
a question mark.

Amazing to see that what he offers
is, after all, not answers: not *I'm sorry*, but
See how sorry you are?
See how sorry you are now?

Mending Fences

It's lunch time and I'm calling *Lunch!*
but Mommy, finding you is never easy.

In our eastern pasture, beyond it
you've chosen not to hear. You're mending

fences your own way, instead
of hammer and nails, you prefer

twine alone. At times,
I wish I had your voice. Your call

across school parking lots lassoed me
and my crafty teenage lies.

Scanning grey spruce farther up
I know you're in there somewhere

pulling hemp one arm's length, making a knot,
two errant posts

assembled. How we used to fight
by pushing from opposite sides

of my bedroom door until I
stepped back and you fell into my room,

looking as young as a sister on the floor.
I surprised myself by holding you

almost like a baby, and you wound yourself
around me. The sob that followed wasn't yours

or mine, it was ours combined.

Oberholtzer's Island

Women on an island in a lake of thousands. And those are just
the mapped ones. Below me on outcroppings, the others lie
like sirens on a rock. Across from us, Ted's island is a lit brigade
of drunks. On nights like these, they bake bread in juice tins,
swim it over, balanced on their heads.
Who wants to see everything? Today, I'm not that girl. Still,
from the tallest limb of granite, between tethered red
pines, I place myself, having heard this is the spot
to get the signal. I make a cell call to my father—I'm scared
he'll die while I'm away. But with hay in mow and wood
in cellar, he's giddy, drinking wine and making cheese with jalapeño—
the signal goes and below me, Ted turns mid-stroke,
drops bread into the water, shouts, *Rain's coming, ladies!*
Clouds roll in. It begins to pour so hard the women leap up
and run for cover. The surface of the lake pricks up, white
water hitting water, and there's no time for embrace.

Breathe

When we found out how you would die,
how parts of the body fold
like paper lanterns, emptied air,
I was struck dumb,
    like you used to fall silent
when as a kid I tested your panic
yet again.

    A friend who knows about these things
tells me Bhikkhus believe that death occurs
when the elements of the body
simply break apart, fall down.
    Except for birth, this is the hardest
act, and why it's called grasping
for life,
    making sense of itself a second time,
the body must remember
its first ride from the womb, *how there's no difference,*
no wall to keep the world apart—

    in these last moments with you,
I'm bound to be stupid. I'll stand around
so ill-advised and wanting
more of you. Meanwhile,
what you'll want is simpler,
a clear passage for air.
Oblivious, I'll cut each of my breaths
to syllables, spend it,

    and when you've fallen from me, I'll think
it's phenomenal,
how the low sound in my walls
is still you,
that whistle call
bringing me home.

Postcards to You

Hope You're Happy Where You're Living—

I'll never spend another golden hour with you,
staring out the window in some Midwestern state.
For that matter will not speak French like a Parisian,

have a tchotchke fetish, bake anything heart-shaped
or covered with pink ice, have a romping threesome
with a married man and friend, get the hips I want

or enjoy sleeping in. I'll also never have a keeping room,
three-cornered hat, pearl-handled pistol, the right word
on my tongue. I'll eat my life with big utensils, thank you,

never pre-measuring my retorts for tartness, I'll continue
to survive by insisting on it. But for your information,
I am not conniving. Nor do I regret

those angels in the snowy park or the best kiss of my life
across from Leonard Cohen's house. Even if it meant the fall
of the house of cards you liked to call our life.

Ark Metaphor

My orders simple: build this thing you've no name for
and wait. Water will find you, then trust

land to want you back. So I do it. Tell myself doubt has no room
inside a purpose. And here we are now, stifling any notion

that we're floating in dark depths, continents
of animals in our belly. Our leafy sails blow out like cheeks

below a sky so thick with sky, clouds so wet
they're mirrors of the brand-new sea. Nothing offers

answers. Only the smallest of the children seems okay
with this. She stares in daydreams at the straight rule of horizon,

makes me miss the clarity of childhood so much. This child, or maybe
it's another child, dips her nightdress

in the rising water. She hangs grey-winged
creatures from the ropes, and they dry into miracles.

Like Stories

In the garden, an edge of certainty
around the last flourishing of blooms,
final reinvention for each iris
or rose. Call it tender and remarkable,

call it heartbreaking,
like the story we all remember, the one
about the child who stole a city bus and drove it
to the Bronx in search of some great circus.

From each petal
comes this sort of thing, following
the noise, the flash: a pleading
which reminds us of another story,

this one about the gardener
all gardeners fear becoming at the end,
a god who's begging to be told
just how he changed the landscape.

Pollen Season

The city weeds are shedding fluffy stuff, the air
Filled with small globes descending.
We walk slowly to the metro, stop before the wind-bent door

Outside the *déppaneur* I come to in emergencies
For yoghurt or eggs. Inside, I know shelves
Of spaghetti, bread, and pappadums as well

As the shelves of books at home—not by
Content or character, but by coloured stripes of bindings
As familiar as familiar skin. When we hold each other's elbow

And lean close, the brown clerk in his pressed shirt
Watches from his doorway.
The sidewalk is plump with lightness, blonde seeds

Drift across the path. Our kiss goodbye:
Needy, odd, and domestic. I feel happiness, and fear,
And hope you are its source.

Us

On this street we glide, float over curbs,
Or sit in metro cars alongside others

Who've come loose like this. To catch
Their glance is to remember nearness,

Flirty know-how, that faint chime in the heart
Like yesterday.

The slick valley of a bus aisle nothing much
To calculate and cross. Instead we reach

Up to pull the bell, announce
To no one that we're going

Home where after dark
We're braver, watching lighted windows

From our lighted windows, resetting our table for a solo
Breakfast, one bright orange next to one bright knife.

Battery Park

At dawn, the grey line of water
breaks against the statue in the bay,
her green back greener

with decay. Smudged-looking wrens
hop sideways, wings like long cuffs
drag along the path. Black squirrels, dark gifts

to the city from the last Russian tsar,
carry on crack-addled searches
for their mislaid stash.

The yellow lawn is mowed down to an inch.
Saplings, small against the buildings,
are older than disaster.

I think wild limbs cope by being incomplete—
lime-coloured questions
budding from bark-coloured sleeves.

Waiting for the T

Under the glass ceiling at Harvard Square station,
a clear block of sky above us, we wait
on a cement raft that floats between two rails—
me, a milling crowd of students, and one brown swallow.

Ruffle-feathered, ink-eyed, she eyes me sideways,
decides I'm wrong in my blue parka,
too heavy. She readies for departure, sets
into bombardier position, putters up, down,

and because she's showing off, makes a clowny
stall, forced landing on a joist. Then up she flits
with one coy wing-flick like a wave goodbye, whirrs
into a straight pin, heading up toward the sky.

I wave my arms, say, *Someone*
help, somebody help—but the crowd is looking down
the tunnel, waiting for the T, doesn't see the glass above
as a human in-joke that fails to get

this bird's *knock-knock.* She flutters in the puzzle
of the joists, bounces off the angled glass.
The sound she makes is barely heard above the coming train,
just a pat against our speckled dome.

Messengers

Under Manhattan Bridge, we're tightly packed,
water at our heels, brownstones turning back
to sand. Yet on the rooftop, the Italian neighbour exercises
his ancient winged brigade. At dawn, he lifts a hook
and his grey pigeons come bobbling from their coop,

coo-cooing. From the ledge, they're airborne
arrows, aligning with the high shelves
of apartments, with the nearly-naked clouds.
The sun pushes itself over the *Parking All Day* sign,
the birds sprout with it, an arrangement almost floral,

drooping in a swoop past my smudged windows,
gymnastic ribbon in a downspin, an airplane's
love-dove banner with no official message.
The cement of Concord Street steps back
into its stoops, lets the routine through.

Ice Storm

On the seaboard, ice shards fall
into the waves.
Dozing fish, oblivious in mud,
die quick, simple deaths.
The not-so-lucky elderly
lie frozen in their beds.
Trees, glass shrouds on paths,
rattle false alarms
then stab
walkers in their heads.
On treeless hills, glass sheets
send toddlers
skidding into fences.
My post box holds a slice of ice
that looks just like a letter.
Dangerous or no,
I relish the rush I feel
for the failing of our world.
It stirs in me
excitement, something
familiar and wished for.
I've acquiesced to it
before, tumbling in my dreams.

Sightings

I'm back in the city, stopped for a red light, reading the off-ramp's
sprayed messages. The setting moonlight pauses, rewinds, what's left
of certainty dispels it: on the traffic island, under one thin maple,
a fox.

In this cemented network of conduits and lanes, her wits
are still at work. To corner her enigma, she inches clockwise
from the snow fence, inside quickening a little
like I've quickened now—

She reminds me of some smart and pretty
sister who thrusts her nose into her task, finds
a pattern no one else has found before her.

Escape

I missed my chance to be graceful, to be a
Weighty dam in place, to be terrifically
Good. Instead, I left you with the dishes.
Wading in the back field, my purpose
To find the last goat who'd eloped
Into the clover. And when I unearthed

Her in the lofty dusk, sweet
Timothy, we pushed and pulled each other
Home, over hill tops where the jagged caps of pine,
And first stars pricked their sharp time
Into mine. And I resurfaced into glare, you
There at the sink, your sad face, without reflection.

Harm's House

Sometimes we startled ourselves, entered
our rooms without a warning label—*Poison*
if taken internally!—
and in one moment, forgot
what painted our roof red, what tied that tight
knot on our doorknob.

Motes floating in our hard bright squares,
we gained gravity and knocked out
the lights. The rattled audience
of windows slipped sideways, sought
blindness. The clear threshold
swung tight-lipped to the frame, grim
to our ricochet
from wall to wall to wall.

At length, the room's wearied pine
wrestled us flat, our arms bent ugly ways
until we cried, *Give!*—
a wail of a word, a word cracked
into you there, me here,
and midpoint our sad room
leaned badly, leaned sideways or forwards,
was no place to go.

Only then did we capitulate, count
backwards. Beg, *Please?* That sweet inch
of a word between the face-to-face of night.

Variations on Rothko's White Center (1950)

On the beach, when we were in love,
we wrapped our palms around the pebbles
to warm them, to let them warm us.
Their good weight buoyed us.

Now we want the story we meant to tell
instead of what's happening.

It is an effort
to regulate everything: the rooms
where we can be.
The breath. The way
we stand and wait, inhaling
as little as possible.

Still, we aren't sure if outside
the lines is where we want to be—

In any case, you're leaving.
I'm leaving, even
the dogs and cats are leaving.

When they ask with their eyes to be excused
we answer, *Yes, yes, all right, go*—

There was a warmth that encircled us.
Once, inside our white shell, we lifted
our arms, opened them, unpursed
our mouths.

That day on the beach, what we planned to be
was simple. We had the reasoning of sand.

Sculpture Park

It was afternoon, our last day, and the sculpture park
where we went to fight was empty.

The path we walked on had been seeded, amplifiers
piped pink noise pre-recorded in a city,

but when we walked along, we were yelling loudly;
we didn't hear a thing. We moved on, scratched the surface

of a giant chalkboard, abandoned a statue of a man
who held a shovel like a cane. A cart of glass perched

on a hill sparkled in the sun, but we were halted by the wreck
of an abandoned car. Arms akimbo, we wondered

if art or nature sunk this
to its axles. Under the frame,

jack-in-the-pulpits, lady's slippers
clowned with nameless weeds;

a cable wound from the warped hood—like the kind
gas stations use to alert them that someone's at the pumps.

If we squeezed it, the car might start, or a tire burst,
something would explode. There's no need

to name this as the moment. All along, we were devoted
to our failure, we just revved it harder at the end.

Edison

Without you, I didn't want light, its choosy reflections
On these jars of flowers, on nursing bottles, on plates holding
Blue cheese going green. It was worse in the garden:
The edges of beans so keenly sealed and alive.
In darkness I waded for the kitchen, not wanting hunger,
But faced all the same with its pain.

I took inside myself half of everything left: half a pear,
Half an orange. One fig gone grey, forethought
Made me leave whole. I wanted what you touched to be hallowed.
It was hope with a twist. I wanted you not gone.
I imagined you netted, pulled back from ether or domed
In still life, caught in the grid-work of clouds.

Postcard to You

Since I came back, my days
so thin, barely there: Peaches,
the burlesque queen of techno-
punk's in town. Tonight,
I could go see her but the urge
is just a tip
of all that's wrong with me.

Instead, I go running
downtown. Empty at night,
the alleys hold the first warmth
of the season in their mouths.
As I run, buildings turn
right-angled, lit to make me
small, soft, and illegal,
and each poem in my head
becomes something you'd love.

Available Light

Before I turn into a spinster, I want you to know
I'm sitting here, where marvels
still arise. You've been right
about a few things: the cardinal
(bred for silence and the cold) did
leave, he took his arctic path.
And I did feel empty as a window,
holding one view—

but another view has come to light,
and alive things are alighting here—
from the rafters
of the railroad bridge,
silken crows, another and another,
float past the silver stems of street lamps.
So I'm busy these days, counting
their flint wings and their navy-black
corseted backs

as they drift into the whitecapped
harbour of my yard.

We Return from Running

One Kind of Courage

Hours cluster in the corners.
The branch outside my window,
weighted with crows,
sinks from the sky.

My room a vault of undusted books,
milk glasses, cats scoring their nails
on door frame, contained
just barely by the dark knob, and me

I am a target for the sun to light up even
as it moves on. Remember being eighteen,
shot-through with what others saw as beauty?
My mind clasps on this, revolves, slightly

light-headed. For too many days I've painted
the stairs a blue I thought I loved.
I filled the cracks and stroked
the risers till they glistened, lighting up

the dark trough
of my house. As the pit of my stomach slams
against its own walls. As if
it could be anywhere but here.

Inventor

It's three, the window a dark envelope.
She lies there, re-inventing
coat hangers, candy lifesavers,
liquid paper, and also a device
that could lightly pinch her throat,
remind her to be gentle,
like she was the first time
she touched an animal
other than herself.
The truth is, this invention is too late:
she has said too much to be unsaid
in the world. They hang about her head,
about her shoulders, words
she should have, could have
chosen better, had she not been herself.

The Good Lion

Yes, winter was hard, the days endless
in cold length. But they were also privileged openings
to further days of the same-sounding weather.

With no escape, I was happy to be stuck. At a crossroads,
I felt something like a god: feeding the loved birds, hens
in the hen hut and jays at the feeder; and taking out

the unloved, those fluttering pigeons who dropped
from my shot, and vermin, indivisible
and quick under subterfuge snow,

who tunnelled and upended daffodils
I'd planted for spring. The mice, despite the catapults
I placed to dissuade them, lived in grainy empires

under my sink. I had one human visitor, my sister's child
who declared me the one who played
make-believe best. I took on the title

for one afternoon; she dressed me
in my mother's old beaver coat: *Be a lion.*
We kneeled on the barn floor.

Like any carnivore, I roared and I roared
for my dictator princess, but soon I was tired,
could no longer think

like a lion. Instead, I studied the dirt forced
under my nails, wondered how long *pretend*
lasts—when do we outgrow

its assumed name and place, its safe shroud?
Inside the soft ruff, I was not thinking
lion; I was hearing the east window

rattle loosely in its frame,
just barely bearing the crow's tough caw,
the last pigeon's tattling from the dark

beams above. The rescue call
of the rooster made me want this all to end.
Concealed in my fur, I rehearsed excuses

to leave in a minute, I offered them
like flowers can be offered, yellow-fierce
with false promise, drooping with need.

Shrew

I dream I'm standing in the middle
of a stadium. Beneath my feet, one thousand

shrews corkscrew and scurry,
trying to traverse the Astroturf.

For weeks I've wondered
if other people see me

as small and weak and raw—
I follow one idea, it turns into another.

I make mistakes, so many in a row,
and can't tunnel out.

Street-smarts are biting,
biting at my heels. It's not what I was made for.

Paranoia, my brother says,
is just one more decision.

And he should know. How easy to choose
circles over paths.

I wonder just how many chances
to pedal back from dark rooms,

into this bright tent?

Japanese Maple, Late Autumn

Full grown, you mend less readily,
but forgive the acronyms

of penknives and new love.
Still, sometimes you dream of giving up
this ground. You've heard that

in the south no one ever, ever falls
from the bright net of your arms.

The Circumference of Marguerite Bourgeoys Park

Below me, next door's blue virgin is frozen, posing in her garden.
Remind me again: why is she not a doll? If she is true,
Then what about more solid things: these words upon the page
That never represent me properly. I type metaphors and ironies
Until the worst thing I've ever had to learn about myself
Sits before me on the page. Oh, pride. It ends like bad penmanship,

All balled up on the floor. To escape, I scale the tall granite
Wall of my tower, jump on my silver horse (or so to speak) and pedal
Around the cement park the next block over. Loud birds reconnoitre
On the green field between white moulted feathers. From phone wires,
Coarse sparrows make little leaps of faith into discarded cardboard tubs.
Bird's-eye-luck, finding gold among the litter. Evening, always so abrupt,

Interrupts my envy. The sun sets battered but alive, I think I'm closing in on something,
I cycle harder, hope to become a silver streak down my juggernaut's stone cheek.

Throwback Song

We migrate home each summer.
In twos or threes, we drink tea with our mother,

then set off proudly running
up the mountain after supper.

Sparrows, I've been told, remember
childhood songs for life—eight tunes

in their first season, then whittled
down to one they keep forever.

As I run, I look into the puzzle of the pines,
seek out these other hardy-feathered sisters;

indiscernible from brown cones glued to branches,
I can find them only by their throwback songs.

Now in quiet grey-light, returned
home from running, I take a clean cup

from the cupboard. Someone pours the tea
and as it cools, we call out

recollections, back and forth
across the spruce planks of our table. I gather

all our different-but-the-same backyards
and living rooms and cars

into my arms for later, when
I'm far-flung from here.

La Dune de Bouctouche

She makes her way along the wooden path above the dune.
She's watching from the corner of her eye, imagining

she moves a little like a crane, but not so necky—lower,
just above aquatic. The insects, shells, and plants

clasp into white sand that yields for kilometres
then falls into the strait. She likes this tenacity,

thinks about it; her body cocked stock-still, daydreaming.
It's mid-afternoon. Her teal wind-shell

fills and putters like a butterfly attracted
to salt marsh. Far off, violet with dusk,

one heron stands silent as herself. Wings tipped
forward and forgotten. The only thing that moves

is reed-thin, a bough
of know-how, a shaft that opens water.

Carve out What You Love

Diagonal rain, cold on flat fields. A beaten scent
of apples, graceless
on the ground.

Racehorses
wear coats today, green padded coats, one
in his so comfortable, he's even lying down.

Already imperfect, you lean against the fence post,
feel the channels of old acronyms
you've carved and left before.

How perfectly they hold your finger or your thumb.
You wish just once, inside yourself,
you could fit like that.

Equus Caballus

I've asked the horses in the pasture for a hint.
It's as if they're listening to

a fence post.
I know, I know, I am no horse. I'm not even
a distant, spiritual cousin

like the elephant
or that other connoisseur of silence,
the monk.

If you can't tell me of your stillness, tell me
why my large, large tasks are large
only to me?

No Answer.

Deep brown lashes hold back
ample black pools; from their nostrils,
they blow mist.

Trappist Monastery

If I stare hard at turning leaves,
the mirage of a crossing guard
in orange vest appears. There is

a kind of mushroom that flutes
upward, holding water in its cup.
I know suddenly why naming birds

meant everything to you. Locked in
your pain, you took to your binoculars
and watched the life in them.

Today a monk showed how the plaster
in the chapel cracked into the virgin.
I want to tell him I already know fractures

can compel a kind of beauty. Instead I go back
to my room. I pull my rumpled bed sheet
straight, stare at bare square walls where

no mirage appears. But dark brown birds flutter in
to fill the lower branches of the cedar.
To avoid your pity, I think I'll un-name them.

Lucky

Today, in his great down coat, my autistic
teenage neighbour bear-hugged me

in his armpit. I was mute, no space for words to enter.
Touch, I think, is mostly overrated.

It makes for only the luckiest
misunderstandings. I prefer the syllables of birds.

Tangible and gold, the oriole for one.
On the crabapple outside, I see and hear him

see-saw sideways on his twig-feet,
make a delicate negotiation with a bough.

Good World

On a dumpster across from the Avalon Hostel,
it's written in both Chinese and English,
and now, six in the morning, it's mostly true

here, where early miracles occur. Milk
appears behind the locked gates of convenience stores,
and women wearing aprons trust

baskets of fruit to stay put
on the steps of grocery stores until
grocers arrive, and down in Temple Bar,

boys are stepping up on soapboxes, commencing
their odd swan-like singing,
while happy drunks look happier

than you've ever been—for the moment,
they're sleeping halfway up the doorsteps, in the clear
and innocent still light.

NOTES

The definition of woodshedding used as an epigraph is an amalgam from various dictionaries.

"Woodshedding (Reprise)" quotes from Joyce's *Ulysses* ("So low was he that he preferred Gibsen's teatime salmon tinned, as inexpensive as pleasing"), and "The Whale" from *A Day at the Zoo with Burl Ives.*

"*Chi Mi Frena*" refers to Act II, the sextet, "*Chi Mi Frena in Tal Momento?*" (Who Restrains Me at Such a Moment?) from *Lucia di Lammermoor,* an opera by Gaetano Donizetti.

"Breathe" borrows a line from "Vessels," a poem by Ian Tromp.

"Woodshedding Is (a Found Poem)" was crafted from the results of an Internet search for the word *woodshedding.*

In "*Substantia Nigra,* Espalier…", *substantia nigra* is, literally, black substance; a layer of deeply pigmented grey matter in the midbrain.

In "Hope You're Happy Where You're Living—" I borrow part of a line, "we survived as friends because we both insisted," from Mary Robison's "Culpability" in the collection *Believe Them.*

In "Battery Park", I borrow an excellent word from Mary Oliver's "This Morning Again It Was In The Dusty Pines" from *New and Selected Poems, Vol. 1.*

ACKNOWLEDGEMENTS

Grateful acknowledgement is made to the editors of the following publications in which some of the poems in this manuscript first appeared, some in earlier versions: *Grain*: "Like Stories," "Carve Out What You Love"; *The Fiddlehead*: "Ark Metaphor" (as "Flood"), "Battery Park," "Waiting for the T," "Inventor," "Power Lines," "Chi Mi Frena," "Us"; *The Malahat Review*: "We Are Really Happy," "Wake," "Homecoming"; *Matrix*: "Distraction" (as "Leniency"); *This Magazine*: "Slide Show," "Varsity Drive"; *Queen's Quarterly*: "Intimates," "Advantage: House."

"Accident," "Varsity Drive," "At The Point," "Distraction" (as "Leniency"), "Conversation Between a Father and a Daughter," "*Substantia Nigra, Espalier...*," and "We Are Really Happy" were previously published in *Neither Apple Nor Pear / Weder Apfel Noch Birne*, a chapbook in limited edition by Junction Books (2003).

For grants and fellowships that supported me during the writing of this manuscript, I would like to thank the Conseil Des Arts et des Lettres du Quebec and the Canada Council for the Arts as well as the Fundacion Valparaiso, Ledig International Writers' Colony, the Banff Centre for the Arts, The Millay Colony, The Oberholtzer Foundation, and Hawthornden Castle. I would also like to thank the community of Pocologan (especially Carol, Dan, Sally and Peggy).

For astute perception and wise advice, I relied on Bet Venart, Barry Dempster, Hendrik Rost, Lynne Rees, Sue Elmslie, Karen Solie, Don McKay, Liz Phillips, Kitty Lewis, Alayna Munce, and Maureen Harris.

Special thanks to the artist, Stas Orlovski, and to the ones who stay in my life, despite me: Mathieu and Olive, Paul Poole, Laurie MacLean, Mrs. Stonich and the Ober Island Babes, Beezus, Francesca Lodico, Joelle Hann and all the Venarts—Daddy, Joanne, Catherine, Jennifer, Michael, Madelaine, Little Catherine, Alec, Taya, Sam, and, most of all, Emily.

S.E. Venart's award-winning work has been published in many journals, including *The New Quarterly, The Malahat Review, The Fiddlehead, This Magazine,* and *Prism International.* A chapbook of poems and translations entitled *Neither Apple Nor Pear/Weder Apfel Noch Birne* came out in 2003. She has received fellowships to attend writing residencies at Hawthornden Castle, The Millay Colony for the Arts, Ledig International Writer's Colony, The Banff Centre, and Fundacion Valparaiso. She has an MA in Creative Writing & English from Concordia University and BAs from Mount Allison and York Universities. She lives in Montreal with her husband, Mathieu Robitaille, and daughter, Olive. She teaches literature and creative writing at John Abbott College.